I WANT TO KNOW ABOUT
Dinosaurs

by Dougal Dixon and Dee Phillips

NEW FOREST PRESS

I WANT TO KNOW ABOUT
Dinosaurs

Publisher: Tim Cook   Editor: Valerie J. Weber   Designer: Matt Harding

ISBN 978 1 84898 527 8

Library of Congrees Control Number: 2011924963

U.S. publication © 2011 New Forest Press

Published in arrangement with Black Rabbit Books

PO Box 784, Mankato, MN 56002

www.newforestpress.com

Printed in the USA

15 14 13 12 11 1 2 3 4 5

Picture Credits:

(t=top, b=bottom, c=center, l=left, r=right)

Leonella Calvettii: Back cover, 6-7. Luis Rey: 8, 9t, 12-13, 21. Lisa Alderson: 2, 10-11, 16-17 (all). Simon Mendez: 1, 3b, 12b, 13t, 14-15, 22-23, 26-27, 29. John Alston: 9bl, 11t, 14c, 18cl, 19, 20cl, 22cl, 24, 25, 25b, 27tr, 28. Natural History Museum (De Agostini): 7t. Shutterstock: Front cover, 5 (all), 18b, 22cl. ticktock Media Archive: 3t, 4.

CONTENTS

DINOSAURS

Words that appear in **bold** are defined in the glossary.

A World of Dinosaurs

Millions of years ago, Earth looked very different from today. There were no buildings, no cars, and no people. Dinosaurs grazed on grasslands and hunted in the forests.

The **continents** themselves looked different. They were joined together like a puzzle. Over billions of years, they slowly drifted apart. The continents became the shapes shown on the map below.

Some dinosaurs lived in lots of places on just one continent. Others lived on many different continents. **Fossils** of some dinosaurs in this book were found in only one country, such as Canada. Other fossils were found in many places. When you read about a dinosaur, see if you can find the place where it lived on the map. You can also look for the part of the world where you live.

This world map shows the continents in bold uppercase letters and countries in bold lowercase letters.

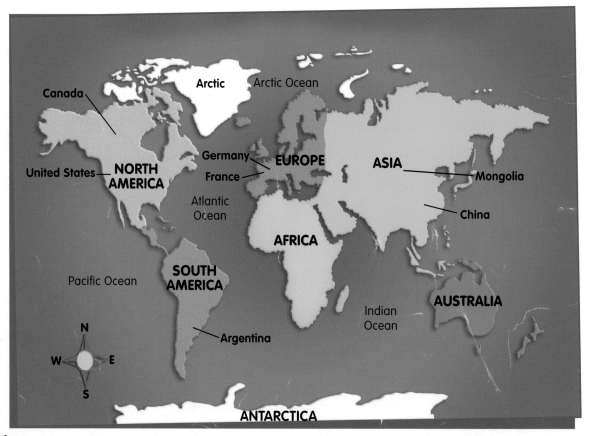

Were Did Dinosaurs Live?

Some animals live in hot places, such as deserts. Others live in forests or in open woodlands with giant ferns, huge trees, and low-growing plants. The different types of places where animals live are called habitats.

Look for these pictures. They will show you what kind of habitat each dinosaur lived in.

deserts: hot, dry, sandy places where it hardly ever rains

lakes, ponds, rivers, or streams

oceans: vast areas of water

open woodlands: areas with giant ferns and trees with pinecones

seashores: land along the edges of oceans and seas

What Did Dinosaurs Eat?

Some dinosaurs were **carnivores** and ate only meat. Others were **herbivores** and fed only on plants. Still other dinosaurs ate both plants and other animals. The name for these animals is omnivores. Look for these pictures to tell you what kind of food each dinosaur ate.

bugs or spiders

meat

plants

snails and shellfish

Ankylosaurus

Ankylosaurus (ang-KIE-lo-SAWR-us) was the biggest of the **armored** dinosaurs. It lived in the western United States and Canada.

Ankylosaurus had a heavy club on its tail. The club was made from chunks of bone. It could swing the club like a weapon at **predators**.

Size Chart

33 feet (10 meters) long

Ankylosaurus means "fused **lizard**."

Armor covered its back.

Even its head was protected by hard, bony armor.

Archaeopteryx

Archaeopteryx (AHR-kee-OP-ter-iks) is the oldest known bird. Its fossils were discovered in Germany.

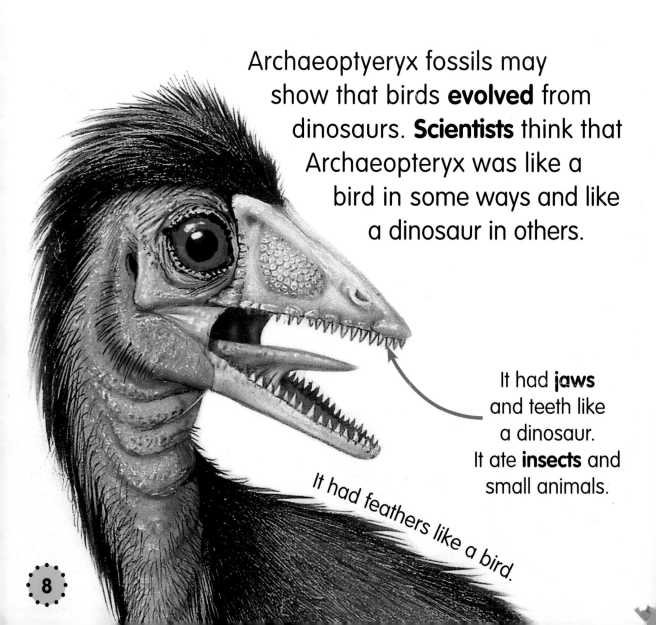

Archaeoptyeryx fossils may show that birds **evolved** from dinosaurs. **Scientists** think that Archaeopteryx was like a bird in some ways and like a dinosaur in others.

It had **jaws** and teeth like a dinosaur. It ate **insects** and small animals.

It had feathers like a bird.

It had **claws** like a dinosaur. They grew from its wings and feet.

Size Chart

It was the size of a chicken.

2 feet (60 centimeters) long

Archaeopteryx means "ancient wing."

feathers

Compsognathus

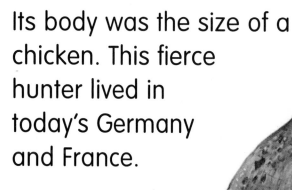

Compsognathus (KOMP-sog-nah-thus) was one of the smallest dinosaurs. Its body was the size of a chicken. This fierce hunter lived in today's Germany and France.

Its long legs show that Compsognathus was a fast runner.

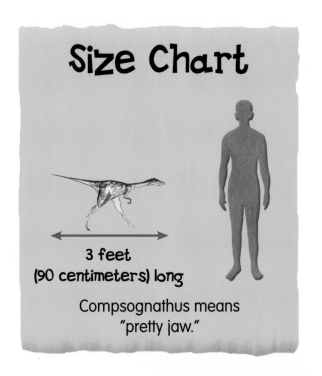

Size Chart

3 feet
(90 centimeters) long

Compsognathus means
"pretty jaw."

This dinosaur's long tail helped it balance when it ran.

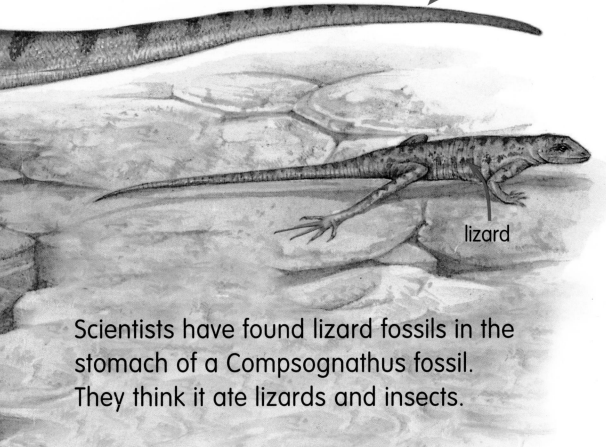

lizard

Scientists have found lizard fossils in the stomach of a Compsognathus fossil. They think it ate lizards and insects.

Deinonychus

Deinonychus (die-NON-nih-kus) was a fierce dinosaur with huge claws. It lived mostly in the western United States.

Scientists think that Deinonychus hunted in **packs**. They could run quickly after their **prey**.

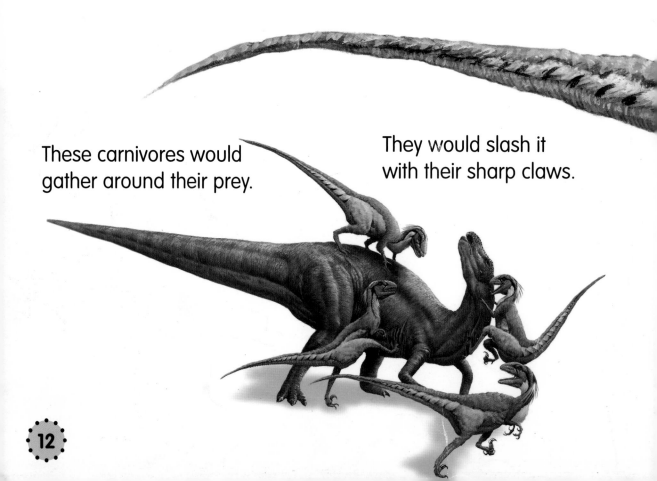

These carnivores would gather around their prey.

They would slash it with their sharp claws.

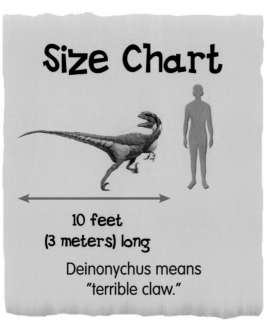

Size Chart

10 feet
(3 meters) long

Deinonychus means
"terrible claw."

Deinonychus had a big brain. Scientists think it was quite smart.

claw

Diplodocus

The biggest dinosaurs of all were the **sauropods**. They were herbivores with long necks. Diplodocus (dih-PLOD-uh-cus) was a sauropod found in the western United States.

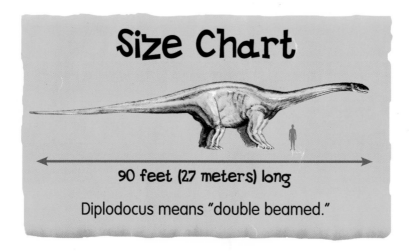

Size Chart

90 feet (27 meters) long

Diplodocus means "double beamed."

Diplodocus ate ferns on the ground and leaves from trees.

Diplodocus walked on all four legs. Sometimes it would rise up on its back legs to eat from trees.

Diplodocus was so big, it had to keep eating all the time! To help **grind** up food in its stomach, it swallowed stones.

It used its long tail like a whip to keep predators away.

Eoraptor

Eoraptor (EE-oh-RAP-tor) was one of the first dinosaurs to live on Earth. It was a tiny carnivore about the size of a fox.

Eoraptor lived millions of years before Tyrannosaurus rex did. But it had the same body shape as the big meat eaters who came after it.

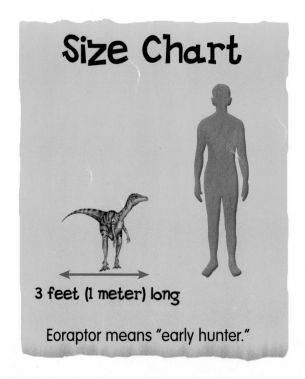

Size Chart

3 feet (1 meter) long

Eoraptor means "early hunter."

This fast, fierce little dinosaur ran on two legs. It hunted for lizards and insects.

It had fingers on each hand for grabbing prey.

Iguanodon

Iguanodon (Ig-WAHN-uh-don) was one of the first dinosaurs. At first, scientists thought they had found fossils from a fish or a hippopotamus. But they had found something new — a dinosaur!

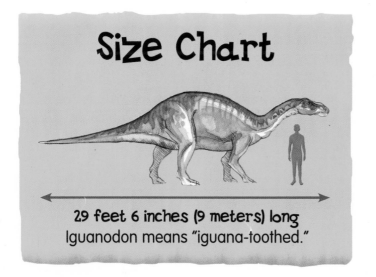

Size Chart

29 feet 6 inches (9 meters) long
Iguanodon means "iguana-toothed."

The Iguanodon's teeth looked like an iguana's teeth. But the dinosaur is much bigger!

iguana

Iguanodons lived in **herds** in western Europe, Africa, China, and the United States. They moved from one area to another to find **reeds** to eat.

herd

Oviraptor

Oviraptor (OH-vih-RAP-tor) was a dinosaur that looked and acted like a bird. Scientists think it even had feathers! Oviraptors lived in Mongolia and North America.

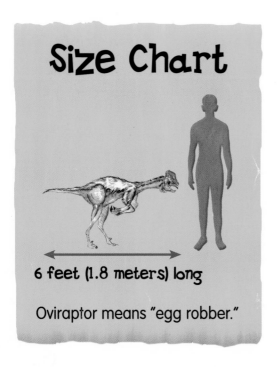

Size Chart

6 feet (1.8 meters) long

Oviraptor means "egg robber."

Scientists found a fossil of an Oviraptor sitting on a nest. It had its wings spread over some eggs. Scientists think that Oviraptor sat on its eggs until they **hatched**.

Oviraptor had a beak and two teeth on the roof of its mouth. It may have used its strong jaws for crushing snails or **shellfish**.

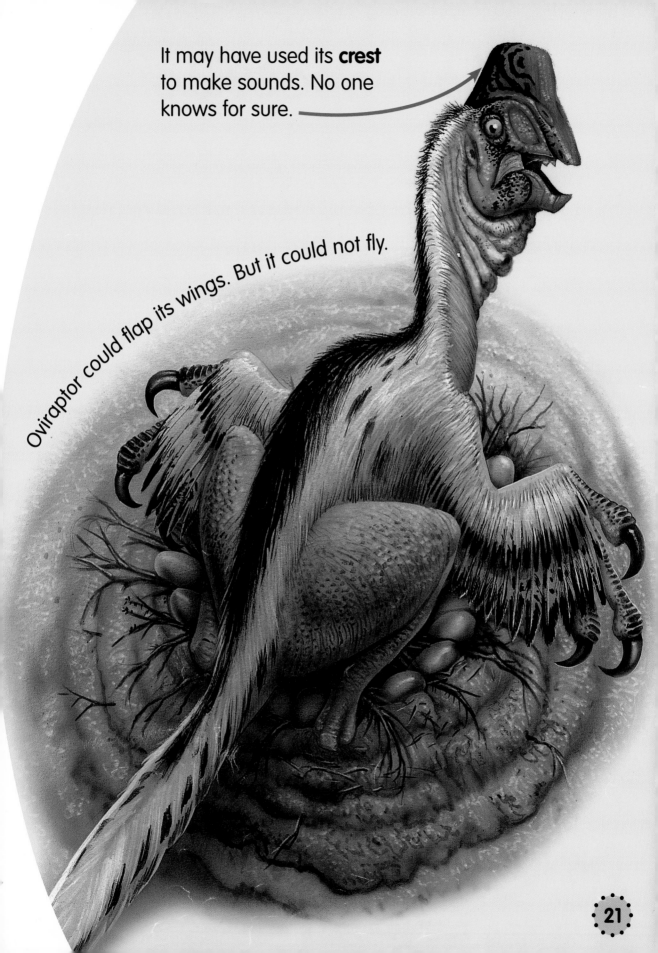

It may have used its **crest** to make sounds. No one knows for sure.

Oviraptor could flap its wings. But it could not fly.

Sauroposeidon

Sauroposeidon (SAWR-oh-puh-SIE-don) was the tallest animal ever to have lived on Earth! It lived in the western United States.

Size Chart

100 feet (30.5 meters) long

Sauroposeidon means "earthquake god lizard."

Sauroposeidon was 60 feet (18 meters) tall. That height is almost the same as four giraffes standing on top of each other! Sauroposeidon may have weighed as much as sixty elephants!

So far, scientists have only found four neck fossils from this dinosaur. They used these fossils to figure out its size.

Its neck was 40 feet (12 meters) long.

Stegosaurus

Some herbivores had special body parts to protect them from predators. Stegosaurus (STEG-oh-SAWR-us) had **plates** on its back.

Scientists have found fossils of Stegosaurus plates in many places in North America. They do not know how they were arranged.

Here are some ideas.

flat on the back

in pairs

in a single row

in two rows

Stegosaurus may have been able to point them at a predator!

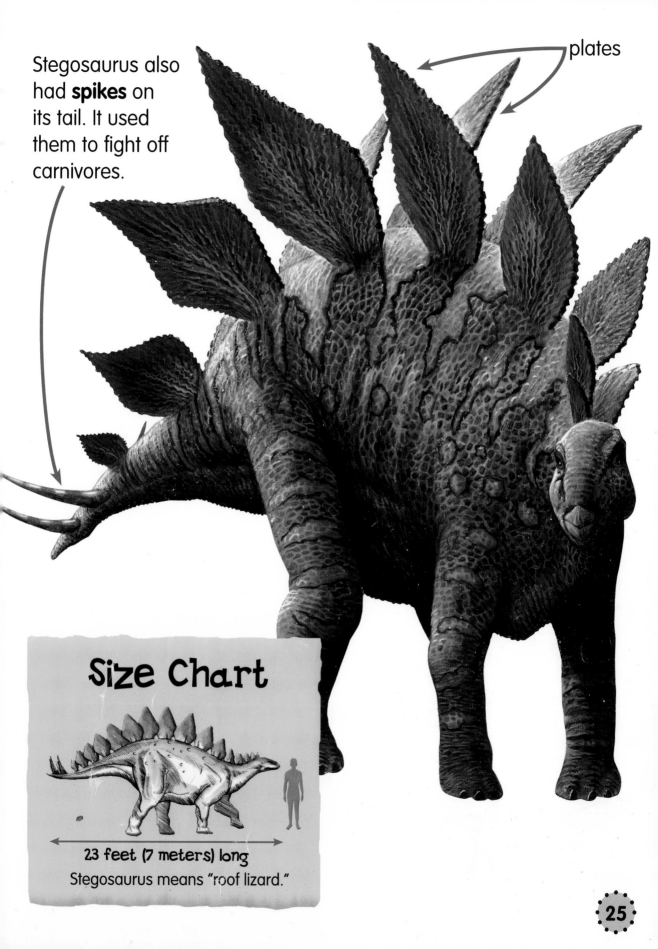

Stegosaurus also had **spikes** on its tail. It used them to fight off carnivores.

plates

Size Chart

23 feet (7 meters) long

Stegosaurus means "roof lizard."

Triceratops

Triceratops (try-SER-a-tops) ate plants throughout western North America. Its three horns helped it defend itself from predators. A **frill** of bone protected its neck.

horns

frill

Triceratops had a strong beak for pulling plants.

Triceratops lived in large herds. If a predator attacked the herd, the adults formed a circle with their horns facing outward. The babies were safe in the middle of the circle.

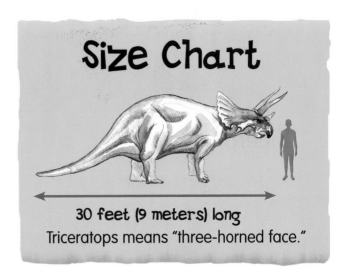

Size Chart

30 feet (9 meters) long
Triceratops means "three-horned face."

Tyrannosaurus Rex

Tyrannosaurus rex (tye-RAN-o-SAWR-us rex) may have been the heaviest meat-eating dinosaur. It weighed the same as an elephant.

Its nickname is T. rex. Scientists are not sure if T. rex hunted other animals or if it ate animals that were already dead. It stalked its prey in the western United States.

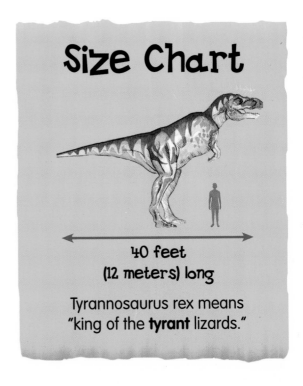

Size Chart

40 feet
(12 meters) long

Tyrannosaurus rex means "king of the **tyrant** lizards."

T. rex had a good sense of smell. It could smell a dead animal from miles away.

T. rex could fit an
animal as big as a
cow into its mouth!
Sharp teeth the size of
bananas lined its jaws.

For More Information

Books to Read

Dixon, Dougal. *Dinosaurs*. Kingfisher.

DK Publishing. *First Dinosaur Encyclopedia*. DK Children

Llewellyn, Claire. *Ask Dr. K. Fisher about Dinosaurs*. Kingfisher

Mason, Conrad. *Dinosaurs*. Usborne Books

Stewart, David. *Dinosaurs*. Children's Press

Zoehfeld, Kathleen Weidner. *Where Did Dinosaurs Come From?* HarperCollinsPublishers.

Places to Explore

American Museum of Natural History
Central Park West at 79th Street
New York, NY 100245-5192
www.amnh.org
Home to one of the largest collections of dinosaur fossils in the world

Carnegie Museum of Natural History
4400 Forbes Avenue
Pittsburgh, PA 15213
www.carnegiemnh.org
One of the oldest museums focusing on dinosaurs

Royal Tyrrell Museum
1500 North Dinosaur Trail
Drumheller, AB T0J 0Y0, Canada
www.tyrrellmuseum.com
Walk through galleries, including the Dinosaur Hall, to explore the history of life on Earth.

Smithsonian National Museum of Natural History
10th St. & Constitution Avenue NW
Washington, D.C. 20560
www.mnh.si.edu
This free museum contains many dinosaur favorites, such as a 90-foot (27-meter) Diplodocus, a T. rex, and a Triceratops.

Web Sites to Visit

dinodictionary.com
Learn how to pronounce dinosaur names and view fact sheets on over three hundred dinosaurs.

www.enchantedlearning.com/subjects/dinosaurs
This site has it all, including fact sheets on various dinosaurs, explanations on how the dinosaurs might have died off, and games.

www.kidsdinos.com
Check out the dinosaur database of hundreds of dinosaurs, maps showing where they were discovered, and play a game to classify dinosaurs.

pbskids.org/dinosaurtrain
This lively site includes games, videos, and field guides to various dinosaurs.

Publisher's note: We have reviewed these Web sites to ensure that they are suitable for children. Web sites change frequently, however, so children should be closely supervised whenever they access the Internet.

Glossary

armor — covered in something hard and tough for protection. Dinosaur armor was made from bone covered in horn.

carnivores — animals that eat only meat

claws — long, sharp nails that an animal uses to attack other animals or to defend itself

continents — huge sheets of rock floating on Earth's surface. The seven large land areas on Earth are continents.

crest — a growth on an animal's head

evolved — changed very slowly over a long time from one type of animal to another

fossils — remains or prints of animals and plants that have been preserved in earth or rock

frill — a strip of bone with a curved edge

grind — to crush something into small pieces

hatched — broke out of an egg

herbivores — animals that eat only plants

herds — groups of animals that live together

insects — small animals with three main body parts and six legs

jaws — the bones in the mouth that teeth are attached to

lizard — a type of reptile usually with four legs and long bodies covered with scaly skin

packs — groups of animals that hunt together

plates — flat pieces of bone

predators — animals that hunt other animals for food

prey — animals that are hunted for food

reeds — a type of tough grass that grows near water

sauropods — big, plant-eating dinosaurs with long necks and tiny heads

scientists — people who use science to find out information about the world

shellfish — an animal that lives in water and is protected by a shell

spikes — sharp, pointed growths on a dinosaur's body

tyrant — a ruler who governs harshly or cruelly

Index